ROMANCE KILLERS

THE TOP 7 MISTAKES THAT DOOM RELATIONSHIPS

Written by
Ali Bierman

"To have something you have never had you must first choose to be someone you have never been who does things you have never done. *Be. Do. Have*"

-Ali Bierman

Disclaimer and Terms of Use: No information contained in this book should be considered as physical, health related, financial, tax, or legal advice. Your reliance upon information and content obtained by you at or through this publication is solely at your own risk. The author assumes no liability or responsibly for damage or injury to you, other persons, or property arising from any use of any product, information, idea, or instruction contained in the content provided to you through this book. persons, or property arising from any use of any product, information, idea, or instruction contained in the content provided to you through this book.

Contents

Acknowledgements

Thank you to my friends whose ideas contributed to clarification and expansion of my concepts. With gratitude I acknowledge you for making this work more accessible to a greater audience.

John Gannon showed me the male perspective in ways I had not known previously. The information he so freely shared allowed me to include a viewpoint I could not have known.

Penelope Beattie filled in some blanks between what exists in my head what I included in the text. Since the reader can't actually read my mind, Penelope helped me to clarify these blanks so the reader wouldn't get confused or lost.

I'm deeply grateful to Penelope and John for helping to assure that the there was not a disconnect between the message I meant to share, and the actual text the reader would read.

Finally, I'm grateful to my good friend and brilliant editor and writer, Marri Champie, without whom my message might not come across so clearly.

Dedication

I dedicate this work on relationships to my mom, Edith Bierman.

Everyone loved Edie, whom many affectionately called Grandma Edie. She always had a smile and song to share. She was generous without ever asking for anything in return.

Through many rough times Mom always did everything possible to support my brother, me, and her mom.

Mom gave so much to so many. Remarkably, she never had anything bad to say about anyone.

Talk abut a master of relationships...

I love you, Mom. I miss you. And I thank you for continuing to let us know you are still with us, still supporting us, and still loving us.

Quick Note

I wrote this book for you, my reader, and for every person who knows the value of healthy relationships. I congratulate you on seeking to understand how to partner in a feel-good relationship and create Your Very Excellent Life.

As you read the mistakes and what to do instead passages you will discover the transformation that can lead to creating and maintaining romantic relationships that fulfill you and your partner.

Even more, when you create your Very Excellent Life together your family and friends will also benefit from the change in you.

> Remember that knowledge is not power. **Applied knowledge is power.**

As you embark on this adventure into romantic relationship success, realize the term *unconditional love* makes no sense. Either you love someone or you do not love someone.

When you place conditions ("I love you when you act this way and not when you act that way.") you do not know love at all. Love exists without conditions—always.

Introduction

Relationships:

Unless you live as a hermit on a mountaintop or on a deserted island, you interact with people and create relationships on a regular basis. Something as simple as exchanging a glance or smile in passing while walking down the sidewalk or buying groceries affords you opportunities to acknowledge other people – or not.

Interestingly, some people, as they approach strangers, avert their eyes. Not sure why. It doesn't really matter why.

People are individuals living their own lives their way.

You want to know how to create relationships that feel good. I know that fact because you are reading this book right now.

More to the point, you are frustrated and tired of not being in a loving relationship with your dream partner.

I also know you want to be happier in the relationships you currently experience AND would like to know how to attract into your life new people with whom you can find enjoyment.

The mistakes and solutions revealed in this book awaken you to the many aspects most people never know—and therefore fail to explore—about how to be in relationships differently from the way you now know (which obviously is not working quite to your satisfaction).

The most important piece of the relationship puzzle involves taking action on the steps you discover in these pages. If you just read about the mistakes and solutions, but don't act on the knowledge then nothing will change for you. Nothing.

> If you take each mistake and get the knack of how to fit each *what to do instead* solution into your life then *everything* will change.

While you may want to jump directly to the topics that seem most relevant to you today, make sure you read the book straight through at least once in the order in which I present the mistakes. They build upon one another.

Start at the beginning to root out your core issues. Latch on to your solutions and make certain you build the solid foundation on which a powerfully strong structure will rise to support you in all your relationships for the rest of your life.

Thank you for trusting me to unearth the source of your relationship stress, lead you away from frustration and pain, and ferret out the interactions that support you and move you along your path to relationship mastery.

Mistake #1

Not Knowing What Attracts People To Each Other

Whatever it is you *think* attracted you to that special person, whatever it is that you *think* causes your relationship to work or not work in your world the way it does – that is not the actual reason.

Your attraction has nothing to do with what you think. It has nothing to do with what you do consciously.

People think they want to be together because they share common interests, common likes or dislikes. They feel compatible and comfortable together. They enjoy each other's company.

Sometimes they feel good with another person because that new person is so different from them— filling in their gaps in living.

A quiet woman may enjoy the company of a talkative man. A man who does not like to feel emotions links up with a woman who feels everything deeply.

Sometimes the desired relationship, on a conscious level, happens because people feel attracted to people like themselves. AND sometimes they find themselves attracted to people unlike them in some significant way.

At least that is what people think happens when they choose friends or partners.

Often, it's the very things people say attracted them to their partner or friend that later become the source of conflict and even leads to divorce.

In the earlier examples:

The shy woman who was drawn to the talkative man later finds his chattiness annoying. The unemotional man who loved that his partner did his feeling for him, grows tired of his or her over-emotional reactions.

So, if what people think attracts them to each other does not actually cause the connection, then what does?

Two forces attract you to your partner

The first force that attracts you to the relationships in which you find yourself depends upon the energy that you put out, and the energy the other person puts out that matches what you seek.

And it all happens without your conscious awareness.

Let me explain what I mean.

You went to a party at some time in your life. You walked in and noticed somebody there you never saw before. You didn't know the person's name. You knew nothing about that person.

But you did know that you really wanted to meet that person. You *really* wanted that person in your life— at least right then you did.

Then you noticed somebody else who, again, you knew nothing about that person either, you didn't know his or her name, or where he or she lived, or what he or she did for a living.

Yet you avoided even making eye contact because you knew that *no way no how* did you want that person in your life. Period.

What caused those strong inexplicable feelings in you? Why did you want to meet the first person and avoid the second when you had no clue about the identity of either of them?

You felt their energies– completely out of your conscious awareness.

Some people call it vibes. With the first person you felt good vibes. With the second person you felt bad vibes.

On a completely unconscious level you recognized their very different frequencies of vibration. You found yourself drawn to one and repelled by the other.

Different people vibrate at different frequency levels.

What does that mean for you? People with high frequency vibrations feel good. You want to be around them. They tend to be friendly and happy.

People with low frequency vibrations, on the other hand, tend be more sluggish and less happy (often depressed). You do not want to be in their company as their low energy drags you down.

If you stop reading for a moment, I am sure you can think of someone you know who drains your energy. When you spend time with that person you wind up feeling exhausted or ho hum or even sad.

Okay. Enough thinking about them. Don't dwell on that low energy person or you may spring an energy leak without their even being in the room with you!

What To Do Instead

Until you become aware of *who* you are and *how* you are, you cannot make the connection that your thoughts and emotions create the energy you put out, resulting in the kinds of people you attract.

You cannot possibly create the kind of feel good relationships that you want to experience all across your life until *you* feel good.

That little-known secret explains why you or people you know seem to date or even marry the same person over and over again. Different face. Different name. Same person.

The same energy attracts people with the same energy patterns.

Replace the pattern and live consciously!

Ah, but that energy pattern makes up just part of why you choose the partner you do in life. The second reason deals with seeking to repair damaged childhood relationships.

What? Childhood relationships? What could I possibly mean?

I never knew any family that even bears a remote resemblance to the Donna Reed perfectly happy parents and children sit-com (or any family show from the 1950s or 1960s).

The fact is, most people grow up feeling hurt or even angry with their early care takers (usually parents). Maybe you heard that men tend to marry women like their moms, and women tend to attract men like their dads.

Ever wonder why?

On a subconscious level people want a second chance to correct that early childhood relationship. People want to make peace and create a loving situation where none currently exists.

By finding a mate who resembles that parent they seek to make the relationship work this time.

No. No one does that consciously. The entire process happens on an energy level outside of your awareness.

I recall a friend relating how she realized how much her boss was like her father. She healed the confrontational relationship with her boss.

Guess what happened?

Her relationship with her father healed too—without specifically working on that daughter-dad relationship with her dad.

You will only see that opportunity in your own world when you take a step back and consider repairing your early childhood relationship with this new partner as a real possibility for you.

If you see that situation as your truth, then know you too can heal your current relationship and ALSO the one with your parent—if you *choose* to do so.

Everything in life is a choice. Some choices are more difficult to make than others.

Of course there are exceptions to every "rule."

Some people enjoyed such loving relationships with their early caretakers they subconsciously attract people who match the energy and characteristics of their early authority figures.

Mistake #2   Not Clarifying Who Is Your Ideal Partner

Do you know, in your heart, with whom you want to create that special romantic relationship? The question isn't whether you know that person's name, but if you know what that person is like.

What does that person look like? What does he or she like and dislike?

What do you want in that person and what characteristics do you find unacceptable?

Let's debunk the myth of, "If he or she really loves me he or she will change." Never expect another person to change to suit your desires or your likes.

When people feel forced into change they eventually build enough resentment to exit the relationship. Even if they do not physically leave (as in separation or divorce) they will no longer take part in a close loving relationship.

> No one has the right to ask another person to change to suit their own personal desires and needs.

That kind of behavior accurately defines what you label as "selfish"—expecting the other person to do what you want so you derive a benefit without any benefit to the other person.

What To Do Instead

Write your list of traits and characteristics that describe your ideal partner. Remember to include acceptable and expected behaviors that matter to you. Know that you need never settle for anything less than you desire.

Never.

Note this example of something I demand in my partner: I like chivalry. I expect my partner to open doors for me and walk beside me (not two steps ahead).

Those behaviors matter to me. They tell me he honors, respects and cares for me.

While those behaviors may seem frivolous to others I will not date a man a second time if he fails to perform those small niceties.

I honor myself in my relationships.

> You must honor yourself in all your relationships as *your treatment of you* tells others how to treat you.

By now I imagine you wrote your list of desired characteristics, traits, and behaviors of your ideal partner. One caution: do not get too detailed in your descriptions or you will limit what the Universe can manifest for you.

You list your desires yet you may not know about a person who is even better for you in the areas you describe. Leave room for the Universe to bring someone who is perfect for you.

Then, at the end of your list include the words, "This or something better."

Got it? Done now?

What are you waiting for?

Nothing will change until you take action steps you haven't taken before. NOW go *write* your list. Keeping it in your head does *not* count.

Take your list. Read it carefully. Make certain to include *everything* you desire in that person.

You may want to include table manners, smoking, safe driving, motorcycle riding, traveling, visiting family or friends, etc.

Really make the time to go into enough detail to allow the Universe to do some whittling on your behalf.

Now *you* become the person on the list.

What?

You become the person you desire to meet. You always attract who you are.

If you want to attract an organized person then you yourself become an organized person.

Get it?

I did not do any serious dating after leaving my marriage because I knew I had not yet become the person I wanted to be. I felt confused and uncertain about too many aspects of my being to want to attract someone in the same space.

Consequently I waited many years to seriously begin dating. And when I had become the person I wanted to attract guess what—with no effort and completely unexpectedly he came into my life.

You see, that special person is looking for you too. When you are both ready you will find one another. The Universe will make it happen.

You don't have to know how to find each other. All you have to do is *be* who you want to attract.

Mistake # 3 Not Knowing Your Core Values

The secret to knowing the real you lies in uncovering your personal core values and their priority order of importance for you.

Think about this for a moment...

Could you live with somebody who does not share your core values?

If the other person smokes and you cannot tolerate cigarette smoke or odor, could you live with that person?

Would you tell yourself, "If he or she loves me he or she will change" and really believe that lie?

Would you choose to believe that he can smoke outdoors only and all will be well?

Who are you kidding, your friends, yourself, the Universe?

It would be a lot simpler, and would work far better to ask for someone who is already who you want that person to be.

Could you relate comfortably and happily with somebody whose values differ from yours? Will those differences cause conflict for you? Will they lead to disagreements and problems in your relationship?

You see, most people enter into relationships without even thinking about their personal core values.

Most people never actually take the time to determine and write down their personal core values let alone prioritize them!

Surprising, isn't it?

What that means is most people do not take the time or make the effort to clarify exactly what they need in a relationship, what they will accept, and what they see as unacceptable in their partner's beliefs and actions.

Without that assessment of values and without the clarity the assessment brings how can you expect to land in a relationship that moves your life forward, is easy to maintain, and fulfills your needs and wants?

When you find yourself in a relationship with someone who shares the same values as you, doesn't your life flow?

Wouldn't you prefer to make mutually agreeable choices about what you want to do? Wouldn't you find it easier to discuss uncomfortable subjects, which are not the easiest topics to bring up?

You need to know your core values otherwise you may find yourself going round and round in circles without moving forward because you don't know what *really* matters to you.

When you don't know what you seek and desire in life you don't know your goals. If you do not know your end point you cannot know when you reach it.

What do I mean when I say core values?

Well, different people hold different things dear to them. Each individual considers different events, people, or items more or less important than others.

Even when people value identical things, they accord more or less importance to the same things because their priorities differ from one another.

What kinds of things do people value? Integrity, honesty, love, family, truth, happiness, fun, health, business success, financial success, sports, etc.

Look across your world.

What do you consider important to you? Where do you focus your energy?

Those thoughts and concepts constitute your core values. You need to know your core values AND—here comes the part most people don't know at all—*why you value those things and why you prioritize them as you do.*

Does your priority order change from day to day? Or month to month? Or year to year?

You grow and you change in life. When you do, doesn't it make sense to change your core values and priorities?

It is all a matter of waking up and seeing your world, recognizing who you are and, more importantly, how you live in your world.

Who and how you are in your world reflects your core values!

What To Do Instead

When you begin to figure out who you are, the real you as opposed to the many roles you may now play, make the time to write down and prioritize your core values.

Know the core values of the person with whom you desire to create your special relationship.

I guarantee that if you fail to discover both your own core values and those of the other person, you will clash at some point, if not immediately.

Mistake #4 Not Knowing

Your Definition of Love

Do you find yourself in a relationship where you do not feel loved, honored, or respected? Sadly many people do.

> If you do not feel happy you will not feel love.

So what will it take for you to feel the love? What actions or behaviors do you need your partner to do (or not do) so you feel happy and loved?

If you do not know (I bet you really do) and do not tell your partner what you know, then how can you expect success in the love arena?

What to Do Instead

Implement the following steps to allow love to flow freely in your world now.

Step 1 Love yourself first

The first step, the one that *must* happen before anyone else can love you at all is...love yourself first.

The most important relationship in your life must be the one you have with you. Yes, you read that right. Your relationship with yourself takes priority over all others, bar none.

Do you like spending time with you? Do you enjoy your own company? Can you be alone without a radio or television (or any electronic device) making sounds?

Are you comfortable with just yourself without picking up a book; are you content going for a walk without needing little ear buds playing music or talking into your head?

Can you be alone with you? Can you be alone with your thoughts and feel joyous and happy, and feel loving with just you without anything or anyone to distract you?

If you can't be with yourself, why in the world would you expect anybody else to want to be with you? If you don't enjoy your company why would somebody else enjoy your company?

How do you treat yourself? Do you love you? Do you treat yourself in ways that tell you, "Yeah! I love me! Yeah! I'm important. Yeah! I honor and respect me! "

Think about it. Who goes everywhere that you go? No matter where you go, you will find you there! No matter where you go, you take you along!

The bottom line is you can count on you to be there. You can count on you to support you. You can count on you to love you.

Well, can you?

Surprisingly, many people don't even think about loving themselves first. Kind of a sad commentary on our society when loving yourself first lies outside the norm.

I am not talking about a selfish, narcissistic kind of greedy love, or a self-centered, "Me. Me. Me." I am talking about honoring who you are. I am talking about enjoying who you are.

Remember the energy that you put out attracts other people of like energy. When you enjoy being you then you attract people you enjoy being with.

Think about who you are attracted to. Think about people who you would describe as charismatic. Do you think they love themselves? You bet they do!

Think about people you have known who may not be the best looking people around and yet, in your eyes and in the eyes of many they are absolutely gorgeous.

How does that happen?

Simple. They love themselves in a healthy, sharing, kind way. They enjoy their lives!

Why?

Charismatic people honor that most important relationship—the one they have with themselves.

> They enjoy being who they are exactly as they are and exactly as they are not.

Who they are is perfectly fine with them. You sense that self-love in their energy. Their energy draws you to them. You feel good when you spend time with them.

Isn't that what you want for you? Don't you want to feel great, self-confident, and all-loving?

Don't you want to attract others by giving off feel good energy?

You want to love yourself. You have to love yourself first before you can love anybody else.

You cannot give what you do not have. You cannot share what you do not live.

If you fail to love yourself then you *only know about love.* You do not *know* love at all. You cannot feel or give anything that you *only know about* yet do not live yourself.

A lot of people will tell you, especially if you are a female, that loving yourself first is selfish.

Not only is loving yourself first not selfish it is mandatory!

Step 2   Clearly define what you need to feel love and to *know* others love you

Only by loving yourself, and knowing and experiencing what loving yourself is do you ever stand a chance of being in a relationship, and knowing what *love is to you.*

You need that information to figure out what you need from the other person so you feel their love coming to you.

Each of us has our own unique definition of love. We each experience what we call love in a different way.

It's natural to think that everybody's mind works the way your mind works. You think that people experience the world the same way that you experience the world.

Let me give you an example so you understand what I mean.

Usually when you go to buy a gift for somebody, you go into the store and you pick out something that *you* like. You pick out something that *you* consider to be very nice.

You pick out something special—in *your* eyes— thinking if someone bought that for you it would be evidence that someone loved you enough to take the time to pick out something special to make you feel good.

Okay. So you buy this wonderful gift. You feel so great about your choice you can hardly wait to give it to your special someone.

Only when you give it to that person, you see he or she does not feel overjoyed. He or she may not even get excited.

In fact, he or she may even appear to feel disappointed—because your wonderful gift does not match *his or her* taste.

He or she does not like it at all! Your special someone would never purchase anything like what you bought!

Here you are. You actually feel insulted and maybe even angry because the recipient of your carefully chosen gift was not impressed and actually didn't even like the gift.

You do the same thing when you show love to others.

You show love the way *you* know love the way *you* want others to show love to you the way *you* want somebody to tell you they love you.

The problem is the people in your world probably do not share your definition of love.

Someone might cherish you but not know what you need to feel love because your needs differ from his or hers. Consequently, you feel unloved.

Specifically, some people need to hear the words, "I love you." Some need cards, notes, or surprise gifts (small or big, depending on the individual).

Other people want to be hugged, caressed, and touched, sexually at times and non-sexually at other times.

Still others like surprises—trips, dates, activities.

And some people fall into the category of the old cliché, "The way to a man's heart is through his stomach." Prepare special meals, drinks, or edible delights.

When you do not know and tell your partner what you specifically need, realize he or she will show love as he or she wants you to show it to him or her.

I disagree with the so-called Golden Rule, "Do unto others as you would have them do unto you." Instead I strongly believe and live in, "Do onto others as they want you to do unto them."

Big difference, yes? That difference accounts for far too many misunderstandings and broken relationships.

You think your partner does not love you at all. You feel hurt and misunderstood—and not cared about at all.

Yet, it's simply because you aren't consciously aware of what love means to you – how you need others to demonstrate love as *you* know love.

Without that piece of knowledge you will never make your relationship work as it could.

Step 3 How To Love Yourself First

Become the kind of person who is so much fun to be with in a relationship that everybody wants to be in relationship with you.

You can be the kind of person that when somebody with caller ID picks up the phone knowing you are calling, they answer with a high energy enthusiastic, "Hi!" as opposed to a dull, "Hello."

You know what I'm talking about. People feel joy when they see you. When you walk in the room they smile.

All that happens because of who you are.

It's because of the energy you subconsciously send out.

> You could not possibly put out that *good, warm, loving, welcoming, honoring everybody else energy* unless you *live* that love for yourself.

Recognizing and living in the truth that the single most important relationship is the one you have with yourself allows you to move a step farther along the path to your dream relationship.

To become that happy person begin by smiling.

> Smile. Smile lots and smile often.

You cannot smile and frown simultaneously. Similarly you cannot be both happy and sad in the same moment.

In fact, when you laugh out loud you will quickly discover that whatever you and your partner argued over so seriously will suddenly become nonsensical—most definitely not worth the energy of anger or frustration.

Step 4 Take responsibility for your life

Who is responsible for how you feel about yourself, about your life, and about the world?

Whose job is it to make you happy? Who makes you sad?

It's not your partner. It's not your parents. It's not your kids.

> You alone are responsible for how you feel.

You interpret events, and assign emotions and values through your unique set of filters and blinders, to everything in your world.

You decide how to feel about what happens, about what somebody said or didn't say, did or didn't do.

You get to decide how to feel.

Therefore who makes you unhappy? Nobody can make you unhappy but you.

How you feel results from the choices that you make.

When you love yourself you really know perfect love. Perfect love means loving the person who made you feel unhappy.

Can anyone other than you ever impact how you feel about anyone or anything?

Can circumstances dictate your degree of happiness, frustration, success or seeming failure?

(NOTE: Failure does not exist. You simply learn ways that do not work to accomplish certain goals AND you learn from the information garnered in each attempt. Every attempt yields a result. Some results match your desired outcomes while others do not.)

I realize that concept of self responsibility may cause you to flinch or even wonder if you want to continue reading.

Frankly many people *no way, no how* want to take responsibility for their lives, for their feelings or for their happiness.

Blame makes it all so easy.

Being a victim of someone's cruel treatment or of societal circumstances poses such an easy escape from responsibility. Yes, that path is the well-trodden one many choose to follow.

Such people often spend the rest of their lives in deep unhappiness, never fulfilling dreams of any kind, erasing any chance for a happy, stable relationship with another person.

Understand that you came into this lifetime to learn a lesson or make a soul level correction that allows your soul to evolve to a higher level. Such soul growth only happens when your Spirit inhabits a body.

Your soul cannot evolve without physical experiences.

Not only do you need a body to grow but you also need other people, other souls who came into this lifetime also to grow and serve your soul's evolution.

Rather than endure anger or hurt at the hands of any individual or circumstance, choose to look at people and events in a new way.

What To Do Instead

Change your past, present, and future instantly.

Consider this scenario:

Two souls exist on another dimension, preparing to come into human bodies to learn lessons that allow their souls to evolve to a higher level.

Soul A loves Soul B so very much that Soul A agrees to come into a human life as a very mean and miserable person who torments Soul B (physically or emotionally) thereby giving Soul B the chance to take the necessary steps to grow through the painful experience and evolve to a higher level.

In other words, that love of Soul A for Soul B is so deep that Soul A is willing to endure a life where no one likes or honors that miserable, nasty human being.

Do you see what a huge sacrifice Soul A is making, completely out of love, for Soul B?

Of course, whether or not the growth happens depends completely on how Soul B chooses to live. After all, when in the human life neither soul has any inkling of the soul agreement they made before hand.

An example is the parent who sexually abuses the child—sometimes repeatedly for years. In today's world that behavior happens more often than you like to think.

Looking at the well-known cases of such abuse, you see some people who live into their adult lives (and often their entire lives) as victims of something that happened long ago.

Yet others acknowledge that painful past and put it where it belongs—in the past. They go on to lead productive, successful, happy lives.

The latter chose to grow through the experience, while the former chose to stay stuck, which means they chose to stay at the same level of soul evolution.

When people say that you attract and co-create everything that happens in your life, they often talk about such situations—soul agreements. Soul agreements made on the non-physical plane before birth explain how very young children become victims.

Whether they choose to remain victims forever is up to them.

In my own life, when I worked as a psychotherapist in crisis care, a very dangerous client went into a psychotic episode, cornered and attacked me, leaving me disabled with a brain injury.

I found myself presented with two possibilities: 1. spend the rest of my life angry, disabled, and feeling a victim of a system that allowed someone so dangerous to leave the mental ward of the hospital.

2. Disregard the doctors' paradigm saying I would not heal, and go get better by taking responsibility for my own life and my healthcare.

Here is what I knew (not sure how I knew but I did):

- I was in the right career; since my very early years I competently and lovingly assisted others in moving through their pain and changing their lives.

- I was in the right field, but working in the wrong place, using the wrong methods.

- I knew there was a better way. I knew I needed to leave that job. Yet I failed to take the action I knew I needed to take to leave.

Along came this person with whom I made a soul agreement. In a matter of minutes she took me out of that job and out of that way of helping people forever.

None of my friends or family members 'got' that piece of the picture.

The person who attacked me allowed me to start all over and look at life through entirely new eyes and an altered brain.

In my own quest to recover, I discovered the very powerful methods I now use to assist others in moving out of pain, reducing stress, and creating lives and relationships they love.

That event, which I could have interpreted as destroying my life (surely it turned my world upside-down) became the catalyst for the needed changes I wanted to make, never made, and frankly had no clue how to make them.

That life altering injury became a huge, priceless gift!

My pathway became clearer with every step I took.

Was it a long journey? Sure. Was it worth the pain and obstacles? Absolutely, as I learned that obstacles are really opportunities to grow and change!

On my journey, I learned that every person who I used to see as hurting me was actually gifting me the opportunity to grow in ways I never would have.

Read the words in the box again.

Got it?

No one ever does anything to you, but to move you forward along your path to happiness—when you *choose* to interpret your experiences in that light.

Your life always, always, ALWAYS lies solely in your hands!

Every relationship you choose offers you an opportunity to grow. You may see only disappointment or pain in some of your interactions.

What if you choose, instead, to look for the gift and the learning of how to be different than how you are now?

What if you took each opportunity to create new habitual ways of being that support you in your search for complete happiness?

The fact is, every interaction presents exactly that chance to you. Live with that awareness.

Oh yes, on the subject of soul mates:

Thanks to Hollywood and the media, people have this idea that a soul mate is the be-all, end-all desired companion who will make your life perfect. Well, that is true, but not in the romantic sense of life being all happy and joyous.

Soul mates support one another to become the best person, living the greatest soul growth possible in this lifetime. The experiences may be heavenly AND they may be horrific.

The result of living with your soul mate is advancing your soul.

*********************SURPRISE*****************

Wow! You are doing a terrific job spotting the changes you want to make that will prepare you for successful romantic relationships. To reward your commitment I have a special gift for you. Make certain you get it here:

http://yourrelationshipsolution.com/readergift.html

****

Mistake #5 Poor Communication Kills Relationships

When you find yourself in any relationship, how do you create and nurture a friendly or even loving rapport? Effective communication lies at the heart of all successful interactions.

When you stop and look, you see that second to money issues, one of the biggest causes for broken friendships, separation, and divorce is poor communication.

Unclear verbal and non-verbal exchanges cause people to wind up feeling angry and hurt.

What if you knew how to talk so others would listen to you, so others would pay attention to you, so others would *get* what you say?

One of my favorite quotes, from an anonymous source, says, "I know you believe you understand what I said but I'm not sure you realize that what you heard is not what I meant."

Even when someone appears to be listening to you, ask yourself if they are *really* listening to you.

Listening is a learned skill.

What To Do Instead

You can help someone learn how to listen by knowing how to talk so the other person willingly listens to you.

- You want to learn how to talk so they do not shut down. You want to talk in a way that never leaves them feeling defensive.

- You want to talk in a way that frees your listener from any need to create explanations for why they did or didn't do or say what you expected them to do or say.

Effective communication lies in *how* you talk to others not in *what* you say.

When you tell somebody that you want to talk to them, what kind of reaction do you get?

Do they seem eager? Do they seem open? Or do they cringe, or tighten up, or look away?

How does it feel for you when you talk to somebody?

What kind of experience do you notice when you talk to somebody? How do you get them to focus on you?

What is the point of talking if you can tell by their eyes that other thoughts are running through their mind?

What's the point of talking if you see their mouths poised and ready to jump in when you pause to take a breath?

What's the point of talking when nobody listens—if they just *pretend* to listen to you?

Your ability to communicate effectively has to do with *how* you talk to them, as well as whether or not they know or care about *how* to listen to you.

Even more important consider:

How do you talk so that you know your listener understands your words and you get your message across accurately?

What's the point of talking to somebody and getting a listening ear if they do not understand you?

If you do not get your meaning across you fail to communicate. Your words are perhaps less important than your meanings.

Note this concrete example:

Do you realize that your dog doesn't understand anything you say?

You could be telling your dog all kinds of horrible things. But if you do so in a nice, gentle, loving tone, your pooch will be wagging his tail and licking your face, expressing pure joy!

Do you know how to talk so people will listen?

Do you know how to talk with your whole body?

Guess what—you do talk with your whole body. Even when people do not see your body language, they still hear it in your voice.

You reveal a whole lot with your face, with your posture, with the speed and tone of your speech, with whether or not you talk in a high pitch and speak quickly, or in a low pitch, slowly and deliberately.

How do you talk?

Do you talk in a way that causes somebody to want to be in the same room with you?

Or are you somebody who, when others see you coming, they run the other way?

Maybe they don't like your voice.

Maybe they find your voice screechy or whiney. Or maybe you talk so much in ways that complain or blame that nobody wants to listen!

How will you ever resolve issues with others unless you know how to talk so they will, in fact, *listen* to you and understand your message and meaning?

People talk to get matters out in the open. Talking serves to eliminate misunderstandings *not* to create them!

You talk to gain clarity. You talk to elicit somebody else's perspective or share yours. Sometimes you talk to let off steam. And sometimes you share because you want advice.

Whatever your reason for talking with someone, stay mindful and aware of how you are when you talk. Note your patterns and your energy.

What do you relate, not by the words you choose to speak but because you, your whole body and demeanor, deliver your message?

You want to make certain that the message you send in your communication is the message your listener hears and processes.

It is not good enough that people listen to you.

They must understand what you mean with your communication.

After all, if you want to be in a relationship, you will talk AND you will listen, right?

You want to learn how to listen and understand the message others send when they talk to you. If you want to succeed in your relationship, you want to listen attentively, proactively, and effectively.

Many people do not want to listen to anyone. So what do they do? They immediately get angry at the least little thing.

Why do they do that?

How do you feel when you come to someone and you say something and they immediately jump down your throat? Do you hang around? No way!

That person very intentionally succeeds in turning you off.

The same thing happens when someone comes to you and you don't want to talk.

Maybe you are sitting at the computer and typing and you don't stop. Do you think anybody will hang around longer than thirty seconds?

No.

What kind of listener are you?

Do you welcome people? Are you open? Are you open-minded? Are you willing?

Think about how you rate as a listener.

Are you a good listener? Do you even have a clue how to listen to someone? Do people come to you to talk because you are a good listener?

One reason I became a psychotherapist was because wherever I went people started sharing their personal lives with me.

No kidding.

I'd be in the grocery store picking out produce, and total strangers would come up to me and start telling me their life story!

Talk about the energy you put out!

Then they would stop and catch themselves and say, "Oh my goodness. I'm so sorry. I've never done this before. You're such a good listener. I don't know what came over me."

So when you are a good listener, that fact goes out in your energy causing you to attract people who need to talk to someone who understands and truly 'gets' them.

What Does It Mean To Be A Good Listener?

It means people want to come to talk to you. It means people feel comfortable talking to you. It means people feel safe talking to you.

When you're a good listener your partner knows there are no problems you cannot discuss—no taboo subjects!

However, when your partner needs for you to listen he or she knows he or she can count on you to fulfill that role.

Are people comfortable talking to you?

Are you welcoming? How are your listening skills? What kind of communicator are you in the realm of listening?

Remember what I said earlier about talking in a way to get people to listen to you—knowing that body language, facial expressions, tonality, word choice, voice tone, pitch, inflection, volume, speed, etc. all matter?

Okay, now as the listener you play a whole different role.

How is your body language—as a listener?

What is your face doing when somebody else needs to do the talking? What are your eyes doing? How about your breathing?

What is your demeanor like when you listen?

All of that matters in whether or not somebody is willing, comfortable, wanting, and able to talk to you because they need to talk to someone!

Obviously, I am not talking about chatting or casual conversation. I am talking about when somebody has something going on in their world and they *need* to talk.

Are you a person they will come to? If you're not, why would anyone want to be in a relationship with you?

Why would anyone want to be in a relationship with you just for doing activities or meeting specific goals, but not able to be in a relationship with you when they want or need to talk?

I am not talking about having a relationship with someone who is maybe your walking buddy, or your kayaking friend, or your exercise buddy, or your bridge pal.

Yet, you know, if you stop and think about it, even in those kinds of relationships, sometimes people just want to talk. Besides, you never know which walking partner may become your romantic partner!

So, are you someone whose energy welcomes people to be themselves, to be free and to seek help when needed?

Here's how to tell:

People say something like, "I've got something going on and I really need to talk to somebody about it. Do you have a few minutes?"

Are you that somebody?

Stop a moment here. The relationships where you find so much stress—in those relationships that you are thinking about right now—what kind of listener are you?

What kind of listening skills do you have?

Do you even know if you have any listening skills?

If you knew about your listening skills, would you even care to use them? Does being a good listener rank high in your life?

It is pretty hard to be in any kind of lasting relationship without listening skills, don't you agree?

Do you know there is a Universal Law of Giving that works hand-in-hand with the Universal Law of Receiving?

And so it is with communication.

You want to be able to give by being the speaker, and you also you want to be able to receive by being the listener.

Or is that also giving? Good listeners really gift those who easily talk with them. What a skill!

As I said earlier, you can learn how to listen. You can use very definite components and follow specific steps to develop and hone those skills.

Develop the following skills to get started in becoming a great listener.

5 Skills That Make You a Great Listener

1. Be trustworthy. Hold whatever your partner tells you in utmost confidence. Period. If you feel you need to share what your partner divulges, to keep him or her safe say so up front so he or she can choose whether or not to share their concern or challenge.

2. Listen with pure love and fully participate as your partner needs you to listen without fear that you may lose respect or change your feelings toward him or her.

Create a space of safety with love, honor, and respect no matter what.

3. Stop what you are doing and give your full attention to your partner. If you cannot take the time in that moment then schedule a different time rather than listen only half-heartedly.

Most people only *hear* spoken words the same way they *hear* music in the background at the mall. *Hearing* can never meet the needs of someone in a seemingly unsolvable dilemma.

4. Never ever judge anyone. Judgments are always more about the judger than the person being judged. It serves no purpose in any situation.

5. Thank your partner for trusting you with his or her feelings. Sharing takes courage on the part of the speaker and a loving understanding on the part of the listener. Even more, a great listener learns from the speaker regardless of how much that listener already knew.

Every interaction presents an opportunity to grow—when all minds stay open to that Truth. Oh yes, as an added benefit, listen to the words you speak if, and only if your partner requests advice. Chances are those words apply in your life as well. More about that in a moment.

Hone the aforementioned skills and your partner will

always talk to you when the need arises.

When Someone Asks You For Advice

People teach what they most want to learn. Speaking as a retired La Leche League Leader (breast feeding expert), former psychotherapist and practicing specialized kinesiologist, I can tell you, in the healing realm, people teach what they want to know more about - so they themselves will benefit.

A colleague described a not-so-mythical service called "Therapist's Central" as the service that brings each therapist those clients dealing with whatever the therapist most wants or needs to learn to make his own life flow.

You see, to be helpful, the therapist must stay a step ahead of the client in dealing with his own stuff in the very same area.

You likely heard me say (or at least read my words), "What you don't know you don't know runs your life." Want to know what you don't know you don't know?

Simply look at your life.

Look at who is in your life and the issues with which they are currently dealing. Look at how your life runs each day and where you are on your path to your dream.

Do you still have a dream?

You don't have to be a therapist to attract people of like mind—people in the same or similar place in life.

When I say "teach" I do not necessarily mean in the classroom. When your family and friends have the same issues (known or unknown) as you, and come to you to unload or seek advice, you respond, right?

Now, pay close attention here, whatever you tell that person pertains to you in your own life.

The words you speak as an advisor apply to your own ears, your own heart and your own soul.

Yes, you say what you most want to know.

Only you had no idea you wanted to know it because it was out of your conscious awareness, i.e., what you did not know you did not know.

So pay attention to what you say out loud. Notice the words you choose to use for your friend or family member.

Follow the advice you share. It didn't come from nowhere.

Your wisdom came from *a deep place inside you where your answers lie.*

See? And you thought you were being a good friend. Well, you are being a good friend - to both the other person and to yourself.

There is one more step to observe here.

Only give advice when the speaker tells you he or she wants your advice. Part of being a great listener is asking your partner how he or she wants you to listen to him or her.

Speaking as a psychotherapist and female I all too often witnessed misunderstanding that grew out of the simple fact that women often want their partner simply to offer a listening ear.

While men, as men with different programming than women, feel it is their duty to solve the woman's problem. Oh dear!

How do you feel when someone gives you unsolicited advice?

How do you feel when you give advice because you *think* someone asked for it only to have him or her express anger or frustration with you?

The Flip Side Of Giving Advice

Sometimes your partner chooses not to seek or follow your advice. He or she may have the attitude, "You are just a friend. What do you know?"

Ever experience that sentiment?

Did you ever notice how easy it is to see when your partner is stuck somehow, somewhere in his or her life?
How many times did you watch and listen to him or her dance round and round an issue, doing the same steps-- perhaps disguised in slightly different variations--and clearly the same behaviors?

Maybe you pointed out the futility of those actions to your partner yet he or she chose to ignore what you suggested.

Sound familiar?

Why is it that your friend hears the suggestion a stranger makes and acts on the very same advice he or she ignored when you spoke those words?

If you are like most people, you put people into boxes according to behaviors and capabilities you know them to have and do. Then you lock the box and throw away the key.

You only see what you expect and accept to see—and hear.

When your friends act in ways outside your definition of who they can and cannot be—well, you fail to see those new behaviors.

To clarify that point, as a health fanatic you may share information with your friend about ways to stay healthy even during cold and flu season. That friend ignores you and then tells you about the actions he or she is taking (the very same actions you suggested) because the holistic doctor prescribed them.

He or she did not hear you say the exact same words because in his or her eyes you are not the knowledgeable, credible healthcare practitioner. You are just a friend. What could you know about health?

You know your partner acts that way toward you.

Guess what?

You do the same to him or her.

You have a choice about how you listen to others. You have a choice about being open to the fact that your partner may be more than your definition of him or her.

Or you may continue to keep your significant other in that tiny locked box and miss the helpful and caring gifts he or she shares with you.

The words you use to talk to yourself about who your partner is and who your partner is not will determine the quality and endurance of your relationship.

Stop and really listen to learn who he or she really and completely is. Remember you are counterparts of one another. Each person you attract into your world reflects an aspect of your being.

Mistake # 6 Seeing Your Partner As Your Other Half

Finally we come to a subject I call the new math of relationships. Hint: it is *not* 1+1=1.

Years and years ago when people got married, they spoke of becoming one. (Okay, many people see marriage that way today too.) They spoke of their partners as their other half or, often, their better half.

Now what's awry with such statements?

When you are in a relationship with someone you are still an individual.

If you give yourself over to the relationship in such a way that you see yourself as a half how will you live your life with any degree of happiness or any degree of sanity?

You are you—whole and perfect as you are.

> The whole point of being in a relationship is bringing the unique parts of who you are to that relationship.

It is important not to get lost, not to lose yourself, not to lose your identity when you are in a relationship.

I can speak to that truth first hand.

When I was raising kids, I was a stay-at-home mom. I volunteered everywhere including the schools.

One day the principal called me Mrs. Damien (my son's name) and noticing her mistake then called me Mrs. Nili (my daughter's name). I'd go places with my husband where I was known as *his wife.*

Then I realized, holy mackerel! People don't even know my name. I had lost my identity. I had become all about being "Mrs." and Mom.

The thing is I am an individual. You are an individual too.

One question people ask me constantly reflects our conditioning in Western Society. They want to know, "How can I keep all my commitments to others and how do I take care of my family (my kids, my parents, my cousins, etc.) and still be me? How can I do all that and make time for me?

And how do I do it all without losing who I am as an individual?"

What To Do Instead

Pay close attention now.

You are an individual. You will always be an individual. *You* are in charge of you. You decide how much of yourself you want to give away. Your answer is a choice you make.

What if you find yourself in a relationship with someone who is so negative that you think it is the biggest struggle living with that person?

Well, remember you are an individual.

> You get to choose whether and how another person's energy impacts you.

What can you do when you find yourself in a relationship with someone who is negative, with someone who doesn't think clearly, with someone who maybe has a mental heath diagnosis ?

What do you do in those circumstances?

Do you become a caregiver? Do you give up your life so that *your partner* can be happy at your expense?

How does that choice serve you—or your partner, for that matter.?

When you lose who you are in a relationship, how does that value yourself or the other person?

Does choosing to serve everyone else by failing to maintain your boundaries serve anyone well?

How do you serve yourself or others when you do not take care of yourself?

How does that value yourself or the other person when you neglect your own well being by not meeting or tending to your own physical, emotional, and spiritual needs?

Stop and think about it.

If somebody needs to take control over who you are and limit what you can do, is that a relationship you want to be in?

Does such a relationship stand a chance of ever becoming a feel good relationship?

Is that the kind of relationship that you want? Will such a relationship last and last and last?

When you are in a relationship with another person, maintain your own identity.

You keep being you.

Nobody has any right to interfere with you being you.

Nobody!

You can give away your power to somebody else. Well, you may think you can. In reality you can never give away your power to somebody else.

I guarantee that your power still exists inside you. Always has, does now, and always will.

You are powerful. And you make choices.

You get to choose how much of yourself you want to share with or give away to others and how much of yourself you want to keep as your individuality and your life.

Your happiness depends on you loving yourself first.

You can give give give just so much before reaching the point that you begin to lose your identity.

How would you serve anybody in such a relationship?

When you are in partnership with someone the formula is never $1+1=1$.

The accurate formula for successful, fulfilling relationships is 1+1=1+1.

Note that another entity also exists in a romantic relationship. That third party becomes your "2" so that 1+1=2.

So the new path becomes 1+1=1+1 *and also* 1+1=2.

That 2 means two people *sharing* that life. For example, let's say in a marriage you have the husband and the wife, Partner A and Partner B. AND there is also this entity called "marriage."

In the marriage, you enjoy doing things together but *not* at the expense of either partner. You do things together because you *like* to do those things together.

You *want* to do things that allow you to *share* your lives.

So you live one life together, AND there is always partner A and Partner B continuing to exist and live as individuals being exactly who they are.

Mistake # 7 Being Emotionally Lazy and Staying in a Painful Relationship

You want a meaningful relationship of sharing and caring, right? You want to be yourself with your partner (and with everyone else too).

The only way to live in true happiness and find your ideal partner to create your dream relationship is to be emotionally honest with yourself first, and with your partner next.

Avoid sharing your feelings and thoughts with anyone until you get clarity for yourself.

Why?

You do not want anyone else to persuade or influence your true deep desires. You do not want to *pretend* to be someone or something other than you *just to please others.*

Once you do allow yourself to see your relationship as it really is, rather than how you wish it was, ask yourself if you want to continue to live that way.

Many people stay in marriages where they are intensely unhappy. That deep unhappiness stresses their well-being, eventually leading to emotional and physical health issues.

Do not stay in a relationship that slowly kills you with stress.

Make the choice to deal with the issues that need resolution so you can dissolve a hopeless situation between you and your partner.

I highly recommend resolving your own personal issues and energetically (and possibly using a ritual) erase *all* connections from the relationship that now fails to serve you.

When people get a divorce they fail to realize their attachments to their marriage vows and promises they made to themselves and to their partners.

That conflict seethes on a subconscious level, interfering with future relationships both with oneself and with others.

The process of admitting the pain, talking with your partner about how to resolve the situation and dissolve the marriage (or whatever bond you share) may not be easy. Rough painful roads may lie ahead.

It takes a willingness to go through the pain to come out the other end—where you and your partner both know the freedom to once again make choices that allow each of you to live as individuals apart from one another.

The separate entity (the union of the two of you) disappears. Ah ha! Now you can truly feel free.

Even when you dissolve your partnership or marriage through a mutual agreement you may still care about your partner.

You may still feel great sadness and pain—along with a sigh of relief knowing the unhappiness will go away as you step out of the tiny limiting box of the bad relationship and into the openness of being just you.

Emotional laziness keeps people stuck in pain.

Continuing, often for many years, to live a pattern that no longer works, blocks any chance for freedom.

Remaining in unhappiness is more painful than going through the separation, divorce, or whatever needs doing.

At least you get to move ahead and leave the hurt and frustration behind.

The past belongs in the past not in your day—every day.

To start your new life you must close the door on the old one. To grow you want to move forward toward what you want rather than away from what you don't want.

Know that if you find yourself in a relationship where you still experience pain, step back and ask yourself, "Am I growing? Am I moving my life forward because I am growing through this pain or learning how to deal with it?"

Or maybe you are learning how to say, "Hey! I don't need to be in the pain. That pain isn't even mine. It belongs to my partner. It's not mine at all."

When you find yourself in a relationship that contributes to *your* growth then that relationship may be worth the time, effort, and energy to find what is missing—for *you* in *your* life.

Yes. It's about you. It's really all about you. Take care of *yourself* in the relationship.

And if your partner wants the relationship to work let your partner take care of himself or herself by noticing how and who he or she is being in your relationship.

Living in your own power and happiness allows you to fully be there for others.

Think about it.

When you feel resentment or frustration toward others can you possibly give, genuinely give from your heart, in any capacity and any situation?

No way! No how!

You can never give what you do not have.

Your partner needs you to take care of yourself to be the best you can be. Then your strength frees you in every aspect of life, including being fully there for your partner.

Everything comes back to the energy you put out (and your partner puts out too) and loving yourself first.

When you love yourself first, you put out feel good energy. And you attract people who also put out feel good energy.

And if your partner lives in the same kind of place, loving himself or herself first, then guess what, you will mesh. And the relationship will flow a lot more easily.

Here is the thing to know that most people prefer not to consider when searching for their dream relationship: not all relationships are meant to last and last.

People move in and out of your life. The important truth to face is whether or not the relationships you struggle to keep alive are important to you.

Or do you feel obligated or maybe trapped in them?

Or did those relationships that served you and the other person once upon a time now need to end so each of you can move your separate ways?

You learned what you came to learn by being in each other's world and now there are new things for each of you to learn, new ways for each of you to go, and new teachers for each of you to experience.

Following 31 years of marriage, my divorce came as a mutual decision between my ex-husband and me.

We didn't stop loving each other.
We did stop enjoying doing things together as we no longer enjoyed common activities. We stopped having fun together.

Our lives had gone in such different directions it just didn't make sense to stay married. Neither of us could be completely happy and fulfilled in the marriage any longer.

We talked about it and we mutually decided it was time for us to go our separate ways.

I repeat, we did not stop loving each other.

But it made zero sense to keep up a relationship that no longer contributed to each of our lives. The marriage no longer moved either of our lives forward.

What To Do Instead

When you make decisions about relationships that feel empowering, or stale or stuck, or painful, ask yourself, "Is this a relationship I need to be in at this time in my life? Is it in my highest and best interest to be part of it, to make it work? Is there a chance of making it work?"

If there is chance of making it work do you want to do the work? Do you want to go through the emotions and expend the energy, time, and cost to accomplish that end?

You need to make that decision for yourself. And once you make your decision, you talk with your partner who makes his or her own decision.

And always, always, in everything you do in life, love yourself first.

That attitude and love for others will change the energy you put out allowing you to attract whoever and whatever vibrates at the same frequency at which you now vibrate.

(You may know that truth as The Universal Law of Attraction.)

What Are The Signs Of A Relationship In Trouble?

So you want to know the signs of a relationship in trouble? Good idea - also not such a good idea.

Now why would I say it may not be such a good idea to know the signs of a broken marriage?

Simple. When you look for something you find it, right? In fact *you do not give up your search until you uncover what you seek.*

> Look for signs of a broken marriage and you will find
> them.

Here is another reason knowing the signs could prove
detrimental to the health of your relationship.

Whatever you focus on grows bigger in your world.
Focusing your energy on looking for problems will make
any *small* sign into a *large* possibly unsolvable problem.

If you spend time and energy directing your thoughts and
attention toward watching out for signs of something you
do not want you will cause that very thing - what you do
not want - to manifest in your life.

Personally I do not recommend looking to know the signs of a broken marriage.

Instead focus on the signs of a happy successful marriage.

Oh! Novel idea. Look for the good in the situation instead of resorting to the default behavior of looking for the negative side of things.

People say that those who look for the good in every situation do not live in reality. What do you think?

Why would anyone call negative thinking reality and positive thinking a dream?

To keep your marriage healthy and happy notice the signs that make you feel better in the relationship.

Also notice what seems to make your significant other feel better. Ask your partner to verify that you accurately interpreted his or her behavior and interpretation of any event.

Do more of what feels good for you and what feels good for your partner. Keep your eyes and attention focused on all that is good and helpful for each of you.

Stay focused on what you want.

How to prevent a broken relationship

When you know what to look for that chore becomes less daunting then you might think. In fact there is a simple secret that I will reveal to you right now...

Pay attention to your feelings and what they reveal to you.

Seems too obvious, doesn't it?

Seems simple but the fact is when you begin to notice you feel less and less happy in your relationship you dismiss those early signs.

You continue to ignore them until the issues get so big and in your face that your intense unhappiness leads you to believe the problem is now insurmountable.

You feel unable to conquer it and get back the loving feeling that you knew the day you realized you were in love.

(Hint: If you did not experience bliss that day then this partnership was a problem relationship before you ever made any commitments or spoke any vows.)

Why does the problem grow bigger and bigger?

You focus on the bad feelings. You pay attention to how angry, frustrated or disappointed you feel.

What you focus on expands in your life.

You turn little problems into big ones by worrying about them and letting them take over much of your waking hours.

You begin to filter for evidence of the problem all over your world.

It is as though you put on blinders that only let you see the behaviors that fit the problem and miss all other behaviors that contradict or deny the problem exists.

Even worse, you twist events into meanings that fit what you are looking for – even when there was no such intent.

Well then how do you prevent a broken partnership?

Pay attention to and honor your feelings. As soon as you notice a slight decrease in your level of happiness catch yourself. Ask yourself specifically what behavior causes you to feel as you do.

Then do something to change how you feel.

You cannot make somebody change a behavior for you. You want to *change how you feel* about that behavior.

Take responsibility for how you feel and behave in your relationship. If you need to talk with your partner then do so.

Do whatever you need to do to feel better.

The scary realization for many women

Many women today find themselves in unhappy marriages. Surprisingly they do not know what to do about it.

Many of those women grew up in a time when the man provided the income and they stayed home to run the house.

While running a home requires infinitely many managerial and other specialized skills, most of those women think they have no marketable skills to offer an employer. After all baking cookies or cleaning the bathroom would not be much of a job in a corporate office!

Given that limited self-image they see no way to take care of themselves if they leave the marriage. So they stay in very unhappy situations, feeling stuck with no alternative.

The stress of living with what they see as no hope for a different future takes its toll. Many of them suffer from depression as well as physical maladies.

Yet there is something they can do. Commiserating with other women in the same situation is not the optimal solution.

People with too much time on their hands tend to fall into and stay stuck paying all their attention to themselves. They focus on all that is wrong and missing from their lives.

Here is the catch 22, whatever you focus on expands. So when you constantly remind yourself of how unhappy you are, how lonely and maybe even how useless and unfulfilled you feel, all those sensations become magnified and more intense.

What can you do to stop feeling so awful all the time— other than leave the unhappy situation?

Think about it. You spend your time thinking about you and how bad you feel.

Sure, you may be taking care of your spouse and his needs and maybe you are caring for an aging parent. Maybe you help your kids or friend with whatever they need.

However, no matter what you do for others, you feel gypped and probably resentful—if you are truthful with yourself.

When is it your time to be the center of your life? When is it your turn to do what you want to do each day?

Doing what you want to for yourself is not selfish. Asking others to do what you want them to do for your benefit alone is selfish.

Taking care of you is paramount. Look at it this way...

What if something happens to you? What if you get seriously hurt or ill and can no longer take care of the world? What happens to everybody else?

What happens is they take care of themselves. So why can't

they take care of themselves now, today?

After Thoughts

Thank you so much for caring enough about your life to read all the way through this book. Personally, I believe this world will be an easier place to live in when people understand that every interaction is a relationship.

Knowing how to communicate makes a difference. Knowing how to take care of yourself affects who you are being in the world, and therefore impacts every relationship.

When each person loves himself and herself first in a non-selfish, non-self-serving manner, the power of that love exudes honor and respect of all creatures. People automatically recognize the Divinity of every person.

Cooperation replaces greed and competition.

Love and happiness reign.

Think such a world is pure fantasy?

You will see it when you believe it.